Scripture quotations are taken
from the *King James Version* of the ʟ

Healing Prayers: Powerful Prayers that Empowers - Activate Your Faith and Achieve Supernatural Healing and Wealth.

Living Word Publishing
4464 Seminole St.
Detroit, Mi 48214
www.livingwordpublishing.net

Library of Congress Control Number: 2015909725

West-Gonzalez, Gwendolyn
    Healing Prayers: Powerful Prayers that Empowers
        Activate Your Faith - Achieve Supernatural Healing and Wealth

Summary "Powerful prayers to build your faith, ignite the fire of the Holy Spirit to drive out sickness, diseases, and demonic spirits - transforming your life so that you are able to fulfill your divine destiny."

ISBN 978-0996372107 (trade pbk. : alk.paper) Philosophy/Spiritual Growth /Mind/Body/Soul.


© 2015 by Healing Today Ministries
Grosse Pointe, Mi 48230
www.healingtoday.net

Printed in the United States of America. All rights reserved under International Copyright Law.

The information contained in this book is intended to be educational and not for diagnosis, prescription, or treatment of any health disorder whatsoever. This information should not replace consultation with a competent healthcare professional. The content of this book is intended to be used as an adjunct to a rational and responsible healthcare program prescribed by a health care practitioner. The author and publisher are in no way liable for any misuse of material.

7 6 5 4 3 2 1       1 2 3 4 5 6 7

# HEALING PRAYERS

## HEALING PRAYERS: POWERFUL PRAYERS THAT EMPOWERS

## ACTIVATE YOUR FAITH

## ACHIEVE SUPERNATURAL HEALING AND WEALTH

Copyright • Materials

# Table of Content

## PART ONE

## DAILY PRAYERS

## Part Two

## Healing Prayers

# Part Three
# Healing the Nations

# Part Four

# Dedication

This book is dedicated to:

## My Lord and Savior Jesus Christ

Who has loved me beyond my own comprehension and who have protected and blessed me beyond anything I could have ever imagined.

## David

My devoted husband who supported me and loved me through the good and bad times. Thank you for being a man after God's own heart and steadfast in your devotion.

## Adrian, Davi and DeMarco

My sons, whom God gifted to me has demonstrated strength, leadership and obedience to God. True men of velour who is not afraid to live for Jesus. Continue to let your gifts and talents be a beacon in the world for all to see that Jesus is Lord!

## Adrianna, Adelynn and Alaina

My granddaughters, whom God has anointed to speak life into others; being an example of God's love, purity and selflessness. You bring joy to my heart just thinking about you. You are precious, lovely and beautiful. Remember that no one can ever love you more than God loves you.

## Alissa

I prayed for a Godly daughter-in-law and in due season you manifested – a gift from God to Adrian and a blessing to me. Who can find a virtuous woman? For her price is far above rubies. Her husband trust in her and her children rise up and call her blessed. You are that virtuous woman. Your heart is pure and your spirit radiates God's Glory, to be a beacon to all that come across your path. God has crowned you with Grace to fulfill your divine destiny. Seek God in all your ways; acknowledge Holy Spirit and He will direct your path.

And to the community and partners of Healing Today Ministries, whose support, loyalty and love is remembered in Heaven. May your seeds return a great harvest and the windows of Heaven pour out streams of Living Water that never cease.

# Introduction

This book is filled with powerful prayers that will build your faith, ignite the fire of the Holy Spirit to drive out sickness, diseases, and demonic spirits - transforming your life so that you are able to fulfill your divine destiny.

Through these power-packed prayers you will begin to activate the anointing that will push back the spirit of darkness and illuminate the forces of light that will immediately manifest; healing, deliverance, protection and prosperity, which are the promises of God.

"May Grace and Peace be multiplied to you through the knowledge of God and of Jesus our Lord."
2 Peter 1:2

---

# Daily Reading

*Scripture Reading To Healing Prayers*     Matthew 7:7-11

*"Keep on asking, and you will receive what you ask for. Keep on seeking and you will find. Keep on knocking, and the door will be opened to you."*

Matthew 7:7 (NLT)

# Part One

## HEALING PRAYER'S: DECLARATION

It is my prayer that this daily devotional book of prayers draws you closer to God. God created the human race because He wanted fellowship with spirits that choose to walk with Him. Your desire to communicate with God freely is important to Him. He longs to spend time with you, to talk to you, to embrace you and uncover the secret meaning to life. It is through our communion with Him we find peace and refuge; healing and deliverance; protection and prosperity.

Daily prayers unlock the wisdom of God that He freely wants us to have. The Word of God states, to get wisdom and get understanding. True Wisdom comes from Heaven. It is not an external intellect. It is internal knowledge that outside of the spirit it is difficult to conceive. But through daily communion with God, He is able to reveal our life's purpose, direct our path and help us reach our divine destiny.

# Day 1

## PRAYER OF THANKSGIVING

Father God, in the name of Jesus, I thank you for this day, for this is the day that you have made, I rejoice and I will be glad in it.

Father God I thank you for waking me up this morning and for breathing the breath of life within me, causing me to become a living soul and selecting me to have another chance to exalt your name and praise you.

Father God I thank you for creating this day, for you are the creator of all things. Just as you created the Heavens and the Earth in Genesis 1 and 2, Your creation is what established the human race to exist, and so I thank you Father for my life, and I praise you that the life I live shall bear fruit and bring forth a harvest that is pleasing unto you.

Father God I bring thanksgiving unto you because of who you are; for you are Jehovah Jireh – my provider, you are Jehovah Rophe – the God that heals, you are Jehovah Nissi – my banner and protection in the time of war, distress, and difficulties. You are Jehovah Tsur – my rock and my strength, you are Jehovah Shalom – The Prince of Peace - everlasting Father, you are El Shaddai - the God that is more than enough, you are Elohim – the Creator of ***all things***.

you are El Roi – the God that is **_all_** seeing and **_all_** knowing, you are Alpha and Omega – the Beginning and the End, you are the Christ – The Anointed One, you are Immanuel – God with us, you are the Messiah – The One who was and is and is to come, mighty in power, mighty in strength, you are the Great I AM, and I am so grateful that you are the God of **_Everything_**!

Father God I extend thanksgiving unto you because of your loving kindness. I thank you for your mercies that are new every morning and I thank you for your unmerited favor that causes me to rise above and conquer my enemies. I thank you Father that you have caused me to be the head and not the tail, above only and not beneath. And I thank you for the promises you have laid out for me, through the death and resurrection of Jesus Christ.

And finally Father God I thank you for your only begotten son Jesus. And I thank you, Jesus for dying on the cross, so that I might have eternal life in the after life and that I might have abundant life in the Earth – nothing missing, nothing broken. For it is in the power and authority in the name of Jesus I pray, AMEN

# Day 2

## RENEWAL OF MIND

Father God, In the name of Jesus, I present my body as a living sacrifice, holy and acceptable unto you. I pray that my soul, which is my mind, will and emotions fall under the subjection of my spirit, by the cleansing of the Word of God, and that my thoughts line up with your will, In the name of Jesus.

Father God I pray, in the name of Jesus, that my mind is focused and fixed on the Word of God and that today I have clarity of thought and clarity of sight of what your purpose is for me. Father God I pray that you order my steps and that you guide me in the direction in which I should go.

Father God I thank you for the Blood of Jesus that cleanses me from the crown of my head to the soles of my feet, and I thank you that you have anointed my head with oil; therefore, goodness and mercy shall follow me all the days of my life.

Father God I hearken unto your voice only and a strangers voice I will not follow, and as I meditate on the Word of God daily I will not fall nor stumble for the Word of God is planted and rooted in my soul like a tree; therefore, my soul prospers and have good health.

Father God I thank you that my mind is renewed each and every day as I mediate and study your Word daily, and pray; as a result, I increase in wisdom, knowledge and statue according to your Word in the mighty matchless name of Jesus and by His Blood.  Glory to God!  AMEN

## Scripture References

Colossians 3:10                                John 10:27
Proverbs 19:27

# DAY 3

## DIVINE FAVOR

Father God I thank you that your favor is like the dew upon the grass, favor returns unto me daily and favor will never cease to follow me and over take me. Increase wisdom and knowledge shall give me understanding in how to receive the promises of God, therefore I pray for your instructions daily and I incline my ears to hear your voice for the direction in which I am to go.

Father God I thank you that I am the righteousness of God through the shed blood of Jesus; therefore, your favor surrounds me like a shield. I thank you that I have favor with you and man, and that same favor causes people to want to be good to me and do good towards me. Today, I declare that I walk in your divine favor, in the name of Jesus, and that every person that comes across my path will go out of their way to help me.

Father God I thank you that because I have the favor of God upon my life I walk in love toward people and I am a delight to others. I thank you for the Love of God that is shed abroad in my heart by the Holy Spirit; therefore, I am a blessing toward others - being kind and affectionate to one another with brotherly love, and in honor giving preference to one another. I am ready and willing to help others reach their full potential, and I am grateful that you are working through me to bring many souls into the kingdom, in the name of Jesus. Father, I release my faith today that I have supernatural favor with my neighbors, my co-workers, my boss and my enemies in the matchless name of Jesus. I thank you that everything I touch shall prosper; good measure, press down, shaking together and running over shall men give unto me from the North, South, East and West, according to the promises of God. AMEN!

Scripture References

Proverbs 19:12                                    Romans 12:10
Ephesians 5:2                                     Luke 6:38

# Day 4

## Prayer for Wisdom and Direction

Father God I thank you that your Word is Wisdom and that it has her perfect work. It is through Jesus, our anointed Savior, who of God is made unto us wisdom, righteousness, sanctification, and redemption. And it is through the power of the Holy Spirit, who lead me and directs me into the Truth of who Jesus is. I thank you that your Word gives knowledge, instruction, wisdom, and understanding to all who ask and you said you will give it freely. I thank you that your Word says, get wisdom and in all my getting, get understanding; therefore I boldly come to your throne of Grace through the precious Blood of Jesus and I cry out for Wisdom in making the right decisions during my Earthly walk.

Heavenly Father, fill me with Your Wisdom so that I will be able to discern Your will for my life and let my mouth speak with confidence, not wavering or doubting.

And now Father, I thank you, You will direct my path in every area of my life and I will seek your voice and a strangers voice I will not follow, for Your Word is a lamp unto my footsteps and a light unto my path, therefore, from the depths of my soul, I will bless the Lord at all times and

His praises shall continually be in my mouth. Glory to God, Amen!

Scripture References

1 Corinthians 1:30                         Proverbs 4:5-7
Psalm 119:105                              Psalms 34:1

# DAY 5

## PRAYING THE WILL OF GOD

Father God I thank you I have the mind of Christ and that I am a new creation through Christ Jesus. I believe with all my heart, old things are pass away and all things are made new; therefore, today I do not look at what happened in my past; I forget those things that had me bound and I look to the future; today, I live for you. I no longer have the desire to live my own will, but let Your will be done in my life. I realize my divine destiny, my talents, my gifts; my passion was given to me for your glory. Your Word states, to seek you first the Kingdom of Heaven, which is your ways and **ALL** things will be added to me; therefore, as I seek the will of God for my life, and I place you first in all my doing, and because of my obedience to you, I believe you will give me the desires of my heart.

Father God show me your ways, reveal my assignment today and line me up with the right people that will assist me in fulfilling my divine destiny. I thank you that as I seek the will of God for my life, you anoint me with power to heal the sick and boldness to speak your Word to all that come across my path.

And now father God, I praise and worship you for being my deliverer and my redeemer. I exalt the Holy Name of Jesus and I give you all the Glory for what you are about to do in my life. In the name of Jesus I pray, Amen!

Scripture References

2 Corinthians 5:17

Matthews 6:33

Philippians 3:13

Mark 16:17-18

# DAY 6

## THE POWER OF PEACE

I thank you that this is the day you have made, I will rejoice and I am glad in it! I thank you for peace; that peace that passes all understanding - let it guide me through the day and bear witness with my spirit reminding me that you will never leave me nor forsake me; that you are with me through the temptation, test and trials of life. Because of Your love for me, I have peace and through the shed blood of Jesus I have victory in every area of my life. I thank you Father that peace transcends my own understanding, it will guard my heart and mind through Christ Jesus, for I am assured that I am called to live in peace and harmony with You. Thank you Father for being my refuge, my fortress, my shield and buckler in the time of storms and thank you that I am more than a conquer, through the shed blood of Jesus, I rise above my enemies!

And now father, let the peace of God reign in my heart that I am anxious for nothing; knowing that all my needs are met, and let Holy Spirit guide me daily that I am not toss around, but is led on the path of righteousness.

I bind the enemy and his assignment to attack my mind with thoughts that does not line up with the promises of God and

I loose peace and wholeness – for my mind is sound. Thank you Father, I am free from a confused and weary mind – for whom the Son set free is free indeed! In the name of Jesus I pray, Amen!


Scripture References

2 Timothy 1:7                                             John 8:36

# Day 7

## PROSPEROUS MARRIAGE

Father God I thank you that the blessings of the Lord makes my marriage rich and the marriage bed is not defiled. I confess your Word over my marriage; I proclaim no weapon formed against my marriage will prosper – Satan I cancel your assignment against my marriage and I release the hedge of protection to surround my marriage right now in the power and authority of Jesus' name and by His blood. I rebuke the devourer; I speak against any demonic force that comes near my husband / wife (state name) right now in the name of Jesus!

Father God I seek you for wisdom regarding (state name). I ask that you give me a discerning spirit that I may know how to please my husband / wife (state name); being tenderhearted, compassionate, understanding, helpful, quick to forgive and kind toward him / her. I pray that my desire will be for my husband / wife (state name) only and we esteem and delight in one another. I thank you Father for restoring my marriage and whatever happened in the past I leave it at the foot of Your throne and remember it no more. I thank you Father that through the shed blood of Jesus, we are the righteousness of God and from this day forward my marriage is whole.

Thank you for Your love that reigns in our hearts that causes us to have a marriage that will be an example for others to follow.  In the name of Jesus I pray, Amen!

Scripture References

Hebrew 13:4                                     Mark 10:9

# Day 8

## PRAYER OVER SPOUSE

I thank you father for my husband / wife (state name). I stand in the gap for him/her and pray for Your protection over him / her. I thank you that you have blessed (state name) hands to get wealth; for everything (state name) touch will prosper. I thank you that goodness and mercy shall follow (state name) all the days of his / her life and (state name) shall dwell in the house of the Lord. I thank you that (state name) is a loving wife / husband, being selfless - earnestly desiring to meet my needs, and highly esteems me. I thank you father that (state name) seek you concerning our marriage and he / she listens to your voice only, receives your counsel only and will not seek ungodly advice. I thank you that (state name) is not tempted by lust but desires me only and I thank you that (state name) praises me and loves me with an unconditional love; being quick to forgive.

And now father I thank you that (state name) is a godly woman / man and that he / she place you first in his / her life seeking you in all his / her ways. I thank you that (state name) have a thirst to want more of you and will dedicate himself / herself to serve you. I plead the blood of Jesus over (state name) and I thank you for his / her salvation in the name of Jesus I pray, Amen!

Scripture References

| | |
|---|---|
| 1 Peter 4:8 | Ephesians 4:32 |
| Hebrews 13:4 | 1John4:7-8 |

# Day 9

## PROTECTION OVER CHILD/CHILDREN

Father God I thank you that my children / child is uniquely and wonderfully made in the image and likeness of God who created them/him/her; for the likeness of God is love, joy, peace, wisdom, kindness, full of faith, and forgiving. I thank you that _____ is loved, is strong and crown with your glory- the anointing of God. I thank you that _____ have Godly wisdom, full of knowledge, and intelligent being 10 times smarter than their/ his /her peers. I thank you that _____ is confident and is not easily persuaded by their peers. I thank you that goodness and mercy follows _____ and your love shines big in their life. I thank you that _____ is an overcomer and that they overcome in every situation and circumstance when they is faced with temptation, test and trials. I thank you that You are with _____ that You will never leave _____ and that You will lead _____ into righteousness, guiding their every footstep so that they make Godly decisions. I thank you that _____ hears the voice of the Holy Spirit only and a stranger's voice he / she / they will not follow. I confess that no weapon form against _____ will prosper, and any tongue rises against him/her/them they will cast down in the name of Jesus and by His blood. I thank you that the blood of Jesus protects _____, every day of his / her / their life - for _____ dwell in the secret place of the most high God and _____ abide under Your shadow. I thank you that the Lord is his / her / their fortress, refuge, shield, buckler; and Your hedge of protection surrounds him / her /them all the days of _____ life. I release my faith over _____ and believe with all my heart that _____ is healthy; every tissue, every muscle, every organ, every cell, every tendon, every bone will operate in the perfection in which God created it to function in.  I thank you that a thousand will fall at his / her / their side, and ten thousand at him / her / their right hand, but it will not come near him / her / them.  I thank you that with long life _____ shall follow You and You will direct him / her / their path.

And now father I thank you that _____ body is the temple of God, that _____ body belongs to God; therefore _____ will not have premarital sex and will never smoke cigarettes, cigars, weed / marijuana or abuse drugs. _____ will never drink liquor or beer. _____ will only put food and drinks in his / her / their body that is nutritionist. I thank you that _____ friends love God and are Jesus' disciples; they are smart and look out for him / her / their best interest. _____ friends are respectable, educated, and well mannered and that him / her / their influence on his / her/ their friends is greater than their friends influence on_____.  By the power and authority of Jesus' name I pray and by His Blood my children are redeemed! Amen

Scripture References

Psalms 91:2                                        Romans 8:37-39

# Day 10

## EMPLOYMENT OPPORTUNITIES

Father God I thank you for You have increased my wisdom, knowledge, and favor concerning employment. I thank you that You are orchestrating a divine appointment with an organization right now, and that through the submission of resumes and applications; You will cause me to have favor with the Human Resources Department and hiring manager, in the Name of Jesus!

I thank you father for the manifestation of a full-time job. I thank you father that you are ordering my steps to an organization where my gifts and talents can be utilize and where I can be a blessing to others. I thank you that my resume stands out from others and I perform well at every job interview. I thank you that I will receive an offer for employment that exceeds my expectation, because I believe with all my heart that You are able to do exceedingly, abundantly, above all that I could every comprehend, according to the Power that works through me, in the Name of Jesus!

And now father, I bring to you a sacrifice of praise and thanksgiving. I thank you for developing me as a champion and for equipping me for my divine destiny for Your Glory. Amen!

Achieve Supernatural Healing and Wealth

Scripture References

Luke 2:52          Proverbs 22:29
Psalms 5:12        Ephesians 3:20

Achieve Supernatural Healing and Wealth

Scripture References

Luke 2:52          Proverbs 22:29
Psalms 5:12        Ephesians 3:20

# DAY 11

## WEALTH AND RICHES

Father God I thank you for this day for this is the day that You have made, I rejoice and I am glad in it. Father God I acknowledge you as the creator of all things – The God of the Universe; the lover of my soul - the one that provides for my every need. Father God I look to you as my source because I know that without you I can do nothing.

Father I lift up your Holy name, I release my faith for the increase of finances in the name of Jesus. I thank you that money will come to me from the North, South, East and West. Father God, You said in your Word that You give me the power to get wealth and that you have equipped me with the knowledge and the wisdom to seek out resources, therefore Father God I ask you to reveal unto me everything I need in the area of my finances. I ask you Father that You will lead and guide my every footstep. I ask that you will open doors no man can close, in the name of Jesus and I ask for favor with every person that comes across my path. Father God I believe what Your Word says about financial increase, and I believe that as I give it shall be given unto me, good measure, press down, shaken together and running over, men shall give unto my bosom and my cup shall run over with abundance of money. I thank you Father that I will have a financial overflow, in the name of Jesus and I thank you that my bank account is full, my bills are paid and I shall never have any lack from this day forward.

Father God I thank you for the move of the Holy Spirit over my finances, I rejoice in what you are doing in my life, and I give you all the glory and praise for it, in the mighty matchless name of Jesus I pray. AMEN

Scripture References

Colossians 1:16                    Luke 6:38
Philippians 4:19                   Psalm 119:105

# DAY 12

## PRAYER FOR A HOME
### (COUPLES)

Father God I thank you for a word spoken today. Let Your Word be a lamp unto our footstep and a light unto our path. I thank you that Your Word is alive, it is active, and is the working power of God. I thank you that Your Word is quick; it is powerful and sharper than any two-edged sword and it is at work performing the promises that You have laid out for us.

Father God You said in Your Word that when two shall come into agreement asking anything on earth in Your Name, it shall be done for them of my Father which is in heaven, wherefore if two or three are gathered together in Your name, there are You in the midst of it. And so father we thank you for a home. I connect my faith with my husband / wife (state name) I believe with all my heart that You will provide us with a home. I pray in the name of Jesus that You will lead us to the home You have prepared for our family and that home will bring You glory and honor.

Father God I thank you that as we prepare in search for a home you will direct our path to the home that you have designed perfectly for our family. I thank you for Godly wisdom throughout the search of our home and I thank you that You are going before us making the crooked places straight. I thank you for divine order throughout this process and I thank you for the finances needed in purchasing our home.

Father God we thank you for favor, good understanding and high esteem in the sight of You and man – with the seller, the landlord, the bank, the realtors, and all that are involved within the entire process. We trust in You Lord with all our might and lean not unto our on understanding but in all things we will acknowledge You and we pray that You will direct our path.

And now, Father God we rejoice in Your giving. We confess and receive by faith a home for our family, and we believe we receive it by faith in Jesus' name we pray. AMEN

Scripture References

Proverbs 3:5-6                                        Matthew 18:20

# Day 13

## PRAYER OF CONFESSION

Father God you said in your Word that if we confess our sins, then you are faithful and just to forgive us of our sins and cleanse us from all unrighteousness; therefore, I come before you confessing my sins to you of __(name the sin)_____. I know because you are a loving and forgiving God that I am now cleanse and is now made righteous. I believe, as your Word states, that old things are passed away and from this day forward I am a new creation through Christ Jesus. I thank you God for creating in me a clean heart and renewing a right spirit within me. I thank you Father for forgiving me of all my pass sins and remembering them no more, and because you have forgiven me, I forgive myself. I pray that you will clear my mind of any thoughts of condemnation and if the devil try to attack my thoughts by bring up pass sins, I will cast down those thoughts of imagination and every high thing that exalt itself against the knowledge of who you are, and I will bring into captivity every thought to the obedience of Christ as you have commanded and that they will not whole me captive anymore, in the Name of Jesus. I thank you father that I was delivered on the cross at Calvary where Jesus bore my sins, sorrow and pain, and through the shed blood of Jesus, I am redeemed. I thank you Father God that my mind is renewed like an eagle and my name is written in the Lambs Book of

Life. You are my Savior, my Lord, and my Shelter during times of temptation, test and trials. I give you all the Glory and praise for transforming my life; in the Holy name of Jesus and by His Blood, Amen!

Scripture References

| | |
|---|---|
| 1 John 1:9 | 2 Corinthians 10:5 |
| Psalms 103:5 | Psalms 51:10 |

# DAY 14

## POSITIVE ATTITUDE OF OTHERS

Heavenly Father, I thank you for this is the day you have made - I will rejoice and be glad in it. I thank you for being a lamp unto my footstep and a light unto my path. I thank you for leading and guiding me into all truth and for opening my eyes; helping me to see the mysterious of life. Father God as your word states, I am to forgive those who trespass against me, who have hurt me or desires to harm me. I may not understand why people hurt other people, but I know we wrestle not against flesh and blood, but against principalities, against powers, against the rulers of the darkness of this world, against spiritual wickedness in high places. I know with all my heart, that all things work together for good to those that love the Lord, and I believe that you did not come to kill, steal or destroy, but you came to give life and to bring salvation to those that accepts Your only begotten Son, Jesus the Anointed.

I thank you father God that because I trust, believe and obey you; I will eat the fruit of the land. I thank you that the love of God is shed abroad in my heart, because you are love; therefore I walk in love toward others, and I forgive those that has hurt me and come against me. I believe that because I release the hurt others has done to me and I received your healing and loving Grace that from this day forward - goodness and mercy will follow me all the days of my life and I will dwell in the house of the Lord, forever. Amen!

Scripture References

| | |
|---|---|
| Ephesians 6:12-13 | Romans 8:28 |
| Isaiah 1:19 | Psalms 23:6 |

# DAY 15

## LOST OF A LOVE ONE

Father God I bow my knee at your throne of grace to obtain mercy in the time of need.  Father my heart is grieving over _____.  I am hurting and I don't know how to recover from this hurt I am feeling.  You said in your Word you came to heal the brokenhearted and to set the captive free. This pain I am feeling over the death of _____ has me captive.  I am bound by the separation I am feeling. Please Father help me through this healing process.  I seem to be frozen with this overwhelming grief.  Although I know _____ is with you in the heavenlies, I miss him/her and yearn to see him/her.  I turn my eyes to you as I seek to find the strength to trust in your faithfulness.  You are the God of comfort, love, and compassion and so Father I ask that you help me tap into internal peace through this time of grief.

Father God I know you are a sovereign God, there is nothing difficult for you and through my weakness, test, trial and tribulations; I am made strong.  Thank you for being with me through this time of healing and bringing me peace that transcends all understanding. In Jesus' name Amen

———————◆◇◆———————

# Daily Reading

*Scripture Reading To Healing Today*          Psalm 30:1-12

> *"Weeping may last through the night, but joy comes in the morning."*

Psalm 30:5 *(NLT)*

# DAY 16

## DELIVERANCE OF DRUG/ALCOHOL

Father God I thank you for this day, for this is the day you have made, I rejoice and is glad in it. Father, I lift up your name because I know there is no other name that is greater and mightier than yours'. I come to you with a humble heart asking for your deliverance in the area of _____. Father God I know that I am taking a leap of faith, and I realize according to your word, that this battle of _____ I am dealing with is not my battle, but yours.

I thank you that I triumph over _____ and it is through the shed blood of Jesus I am delivered, redeemed and set free from _____. I thank you that I will no longer have a desire for _____ and _____ has no dominion over me.

I thank you Father that whatever _____ has done to my body as a result of the abuse, I thank you that my body have been restored back to its original state. I speak over my body, I believe that every tissue, every organ, every muscle, every cell will function in the perfection in which you created it to function in and from this day forward, I have been made whole; nothing missing, nothing broken, in the power and authority of Jesus' name, Amen!

Scripture Reference

Romans 7:6                                        Romans 8:21

―――――◆―――――

# Daily Reading

*Scripture Reading To Healing Prayers*        John 15:9-17

*"As the Father has loved me so have I loved you. Now remain in my love. If you obey my commands, you will remain in my love, just as I have obeyed my father's commands and remain in His love. I have told you this so that my joy may be in you and that your joy may be complete."*

John 15:9-17 (NIV)

# DAY 17

## DELIVERANCE OF DEMONIC FORCES

Heavenly Father, in the name of Jesus Christ, I believe you are the God that created heaven and earth and is the God that rule over all in this present world, the underworld and the heavens. It is through the shed blood of Jesus I am able to approach your throne of grace and ask for your help in the time of need.

I confess to you Father that I am living in sin and have opened the door to be attacked by demonic spirits. Because of your love through the death and resurrection power of Jesus Christ I ask for your forgiveness. Your Word says that if I confess my sins you are faithful and just to forgive me of my sins and cleanse me of **ALL** unrighteousness; therefore Father I believe with all my heart I am forgiven and I release my faith for your protection and deliverance from these demonic spirits that is trying to overtake me and destroy me. You said in your Word that the thief comes to steal, kill and destroy, but you come to bring life; therefore choose life that me and my seed shall live. I stand before you right now Father God and I choose you Jesus as Lord of my life – my redeemer, and from this day forward I stand in authority over demonic spirits. I understand that I do not wrestle against flesh and blood but against principalities, against powers, against the rulers of the darkness of this present world, against spiritual wickedness in high places, and for this reason, I put on the whole armor of God that I may be able to stand against the wiles of the devil; from every evil spirit and evil influence afflicting my life. I humbly ask to seek your presence, and pray for the wisdom and power of your Holy Spirit, and the presence of your Holy Angels to help in this matter. Illuminate my mind with the truth and teach me to war against this evil intrusion and lead me into victory of your precious Son, Jesus Christ my Savior, whose blood was shed for me over 2000 years ago, to deliver and set me free from the power of sin, Satan and his kingdom of darkness.

I plead the blood of Jesus Christ over my life right now. I say with a loud voice I am redeemed, made justified, cleansed and sanctified by the blood of Jesus Christ and His Holy Name. Amen!

Scripture References

Ephesians 3:20                          Isaiah 54:17
2Corinthians 2:14

# DAY 18

## REMOVAL OF DEBT

Father God I lift you up this day, because you are high and lifted above the Earth and all the Earth praises your great and majestic name. I thank you that you have equipped me with everything I need and caused me to triumph in every area of my life. I thank you for delivering me from the curse of debt through the power and authority of the name of Jesus, and my desire to indulge in excessive spending and living above my means cease this day.

Father God I thank you that you give me daily bread to enrich my spirit and empower my soul. As your Word says to seek Godly wisdom in the area of my finances, I seek the power of wisdom and I get understanding regarding how to manage my finances. I thank you for the debt removing, yolk destroying, power of God on my life and I thank you for supernatural removal of all debt in the mighty name of Jesus.

And now Father God, I speak multiplication over my finances, I call those things to be not as though they were and I believe with all my heart I am blessed in my household, on my job, my bank account overflows and I have more than enough to supply my every need and desire; in the name of Jesus I pray. Amen!

# Daily Reading

*Scripture Reading for Healing Prayers*        Isaiah 40:12-31

*"But those who hope in the Lord will renew their strength. They will soar on wings like eagles; they will run and not grow weary, they will walk and not be faint."*

Isaiah 40:31 (NIV)

# PART TWO

## HEALING PRAYERS

In the early 1990's I sought God regarding my ministry. I knew I had a special anointing on my life but, I could not exactly place my finger on it. In mid June of 1997, I attended a 5-day Healing Conference. As the healing anointing fell on the speaker that night, I watched how many came to the Alter for healing. I was astonished by the sickness and diseases that crippled believers – those that loved God, but yet was bound in chains by Satan. That old devil had put sickness and disease on God's people and blinded believers into thinking that this was there life and healing was not for them. I was moved with compassion not only to see the condition my Christian brothers and sisters were in, but to eventually see the miraculous take place – The Holy Spirit revealed himself to me, but more importantly to those that received their healing that night. People stood up out of their wheel chairs and walking canes were tossed to the side as God's people shouted in victory over sickness and death. Glory to God!

From that day forward, I knew my assignment. That night God showed me a vision, breathe the healing anointing on me and as I received the Power of God to heal the sick and broken hearted, I have been proclaiming the victory over death every sense that day – Hallelujah the curse is broken; through the anointed power of the Name of Jesus!

The Word of God is alive! It is powerful and sharper than any two-edged sword. As we speak the Word of God it will not return void but will go forth to accomplish what we believe it will accomplish. Words are powerful. It was through The Word, this world was created. God spoke and the manifestation of what He spoke appeared. The Word of God states that "He sent His Word, and healed them, and delivered them from death".

As you confess these healing prayers over your body, allow the Word to saturate your mind and body – destroying the attacks of the enemy, in the Name of Jesus!

# LETTING GO OF RESENTMENT & BITTERNESS

Dear Heavenly Father, I thank you that you crowned me with Your Glory and clothed me with Your Grace. I thank you that Your Word is truth; it is a lamp unto my footsteps and a light to my path; it is removing every burden and destroying every yoke; bring peace and comfort to my spirit. You said in Your Word that Your yoke is easy and Your burden is light; therefore as I meditate Your Word daily, my mind is being transformed and renewed from negative thoughts and as a result, I let go of resentment and bitterness towards those that has hurt me. I realize that as I whole on to the hurt in my heart, I am giving the devil place in my mind and power over my life; therefore I take back that power and control, and I cast my cares upon you; for I know you care for me. It is Your love that causes me to rise above my enemies and Your Grace that I have victory. I realize this walk is a walk of faith and that this road will not be easy, but in my weakness; You makes me strong, and through my temptation, test and trials You give me peace; that peace, which surpasses all understanding, it will guard my heart and mind in Christ Jesus.

You said in Your Word to be angry but do not sin; to do not let the sun go down on my anger, and give no opportunity to the devil; to do not be overcome by evil, but overcome evil with good; therefore I thank you that you help me to overcome resentment and bitterness towards those that has hurt me. And as I come to You Father, according to Your Word, being weary and heavy burden, You will give me rest. Thank you for helping me to let go resentment and bitterness. I trust in You Lord with all my heart, and I lean not on my own understanding, but in all my ways I acknowledge You and You directs my path. In Jesus' Name I pray – Amen!

Scripture References

Psalms 5:12                           Isaiah 10:27
2 Corinthians 12:9-11                 Colossians 3:13

## HEALING FROM CANCER / DISEASES / SICKNESS

Father God I thank you for Your only begotten Son Jesus, who died for me on the cross, that I may have life and have it more abundantly. I thank you Father God for Jesus who borne my grief's, my sickness and infirmities, and all diseases, and carried my sorrow on the cross. He was wounded for my transgressions and bruised for my iniquities; the chastisement of my peace was upon Him and by His stripes I was healed that day on the cross, from the crown of my head to the soles of my feet. Father God I thank you for Jesus' shed blood that washed all my sins away and I thank you for the death and resurrection of Jesus Christ the anointed one – my redeemer.

Father God I believe with all my heart, the day of Jesus' crucifixion was the day I was delivered from this disease called Cancer. I release my faith right now and I speak to Cancer – for everything that has a name must bow down to the Name of Jesus; for I believe there is Power in the Name of Jesus; therefore in the Power and Authority of Jesus' Name I say Spirit of Cancer you must go out of my body now! I command you Cancer to be destroyed. I deactivate your power and I destroy your assignment against me; for through the shed blood of Jesus I am healed, I am delivered and I am made whole! Nothing missing, nothing broken in my life; for I am restored back to complete health – in the Name of Jesus!

Father God, I believe you are Jehovah Rapha - the God that heals. I believe You sent Your Word (Jesus) to heal all diseases, therefore to those that receive Jesus receives the promises of God. I receive Jesus, I believe He is the Son of God and I believe He rose from the grave and all power was given to Him in the Heavens and in the Earth. Because I believe, I receive my healing now! Thank you Father for my healing and I rejoice in the victory over death.

And now Father God I give you all the Glory and Praise for my complete deliverance. I neither look unto the left nor the right but my eyes are fixed on You who is the author and finisher of my faith, and the only report I believe is the report of the Lord that says; I am healed, I am delivered, I am filled, I am free – I have the victory! By the power and authority in the Holy Name of Jesus, Amen!

Scripture Reference

1 Corinthians 15-54-57                    Isaiah 53:4-5

# PRAYER FOR A SUCCESSFUL SURGERY

Father God I thank you for this day for this is the day you have made, I rejoice and is glad in it. Father God I thank you for Your Word, for I know that Your Word is a lamp unto my footstep and a light unto my path. I believe with all my heart that Your Word is alive, it is active, and is the working Power of God. I thank you that Your Word is quick; it is powerful and sharper than any two-edged sword and it is at work performing the promises that You have laid out for me.

Father I believe with all my heart that the death and resurrection of Jesus Christ the Anointed One and through His shed blood I was healed that day on the cross. Nonetheless, Father I pray for the manifestation of Your healing and deliverance right now during this surgery. I release my faith for a successful surgery. I give you total charge over the procedure and I pray that the doctors and nurses in the operating room follow your instructions during the procedure. I release my Angels right now, and I command them to go forth and make preparation for a successful surgery. Holy Spirit bring me comfort and peace, and minister to me during this surgery; bring me songs, hymns and melodies as a sign that you are with me.

And now father God, I thank you for a successful surgery and a quick recovery. I thank you that my health is renewed and my body is stronger each passing day, in the name of Jesus! Amen

Scripture References

Hebrews 4:12                                    Isaiah 53:4-5

# HEALING OVER A BROKEN HEART

Father God I thank you for Your Love that shines big in my life. You said in Your Word that you came to heal the brokenhearted and bind up those in sorrow. For St. John 3:16 states, for You so loved me that you gave your only begotten Son Jesus that whosoever believes in Him will not perish but have everlasting life. Father God I thank you that it was through your love my heart no longer grieves and hurt. I thank you that it is Your saving grace that I am redeemed and through your blood I am healed, nothing missing - nothing broken. I thank you Father that it is the love of God that is shed abroad in my heart by the Holy Spirit that causes me to be uplifted and inspired from the many years I suffered from a broken heart, I am grateful that I can turn to you as the lover of my soul and my healer.

I thank you for giving me Holy Spirit to comfort me when I am down and speaking to me softly when I feel lonely.

I thank you father for delivering me out of the darkness of sorrow into your marvelous light. I thank you father that you have turned my mourning into dancing and my sorrow into joy.

Father I thank you for mending my broken heart and renewing my mind that I no longer have a victim mentality but a victorious mentality. From this day forward, I look not at the thing (s) that had me bound, but I press forward to all things that are lovely and kind. I forgive those that hurt me and I pray for my enemies because I am released from bondage - the chains that had me bound is broken, in the Name of Jesus! Amen.

Scripture References

Ephesians 2:8                              John 14:16
Psalms 30:11-12                           Psalms 147:3

# CASTING DOWN WRONGFUL THOUGHTS

Father God you are my healer and my deliverer, therefore I whole every thought and imagination that is pure, holy and just, and I cast down any thoughts that is contrary to what your Word says about me and the provisions that is promised to me before the foundation of the world was created. Your Word says I am the head and not the tail, I am above only and not beneath for greater is He who lives in me then he who lives in the world!

Your Word further says that I was created in Your Image and in Your likeness, therefore I have the mind of Christ, I am anointed to prosper and I have the power to rise above my enemies – those that try to come against me and speak evil towards me. I thank you Father that as I mediate your

Word daily, that I dwell in the secret place of the Most High God and I will abide under your shadow, for I will say of the Lord you are my refuge, my fortress, my God in You and only You I will trust. I thank you Father that because my mind is stayed on you that I shall be like a tree planted by the rivers of waters that brings forth fruit in my season, and I am confident that I shall neither slumber nor sleep; because you said you will be with me always.

I thank you Father God that when I am weak You restore my soul, when I don't know which way to go, you will lead me in the path of righteousness for your name sake. I thank you Father that you causes me to walk through the shadow of the valley of darkness but because you said you will never leave me nor forsake me, I fear no evil for I know you are with me, your rod and staff comforts me, you prepare everything I need before the presence of my enemies. I am with assurance that goodness and mercy will follow me all the days of my life and I thank you that I will dwell in the house of the Lord forever, and I thank you father that as I mediate on your Word day and night it protects me and renews my mind from anything that is contrary to what Your Word says about me and the provisions that you promised me as a seed of Abraham and a son/daughter of the Most High God - my High Priest; my mind and thoughts are stayed on you. In the power and authority of Jesus' name, Amen!

Scripture References

Psalms 23:1-6                              Psalms 121:4

# PART THREE

## HEALING THE NATIONS

God made a proclamation that Israel is His chosen land for His Children - The Christian Jews; therefore, every tribe of Israel is to possess it. The Word of God states, those that bless Israel will be blessed and those that curse Israel will be cursed.

Israel is the Holy Land of God and King Solomon's (The Jewish) Temple in Jerusalem belongs to God. Israel's enemy, namely Syria, Iran and Turkey is making every attempt to take possession of it, but your prayers will hold back the demonic forces that are coming against Israel.

Please join me in prayer for Israel and the United States. Pray that the United States will continue to support Israel – being the armor that it was created to be and the financial support it needs to win over the attack of their enemy: Syria, Iran and Turkey. Pray that Israel do not attempt to compromise their value system with Syria, Iran and Turkey, but will stand strong believing that God is with them. Amen

# Daily Reading

*Scripture Reading To Healing Prayers*           2 Timothy 2: 1-7

*"I urge, then, first of all, that petitions, prayers, intercession and thanksgiving be made for all people— for kings and all those in authority, that we may live peaceful and quiet lives in all godliness and holiness. This is good, and pleases God our Savior, who wants all people to be saved and to come to a knowledge of the truth. For there is one God and one mediator between God and mankind, the man Christ Jesus."*

2 Timothy 2: 1-7

## PRAYER OVER THE UNITED STATES OF AMERICA

Dear Heavenly Father, I lift up the United States of America, the President of this country, its' Officials and The Supreme Court Justices. I pray that you continue to place a hedge of protection around the entire country of the USA. I thank you that no hurt, harm or danger will come to this country and that our Government will obey your commandments. I pray that you reveal yourself to the President, its' Officials and The Supreme Court Justices, and that you steer them in the right direction according to the foundation of the Word of God and that they will no longer look unto the left or right but unto You for guidance when making decisions regarding this Country and the Nation of Israel.

Father God I come to your Throne of Grace as your Beloved Child through the shed blood of Jesus Christ to ask for Mercy as I stand in the gap for the United States of America.

I ask for your forgiveness for the sin that has taken whole over the United States; sin of adultery, sin of rebellion, sin of idolatry, sin of homosexuality, sin of deception; lying, greed, hands that shed innocent blood, a heart that devises wicked schemes, feet that are quick to rush into evil, Political leadership that is pouring out lies for their self indulgence and to deceive the community, and those that has denounced your begotten Son Jesus - all are an abomination to you according to Proverbs 6:16-19. I believe with all my heart that if the saints pray for forgiveness, you will whole back destruction, therefore, let your mercy be upon the United States of America.

I pray that you will put in place Godly Officials and Supreme Court Justices that is obedient to Your Word – using Godly principles as the United States law book when making decisions and will not allow fear of man to dictate what this country's creed will follow.

And now Father, I thank you that you are our shield; the glory and the lifter of our head. Amen!


- God Bless America -

# Prayer over the Nation Israel

Dear Heavenly Father, I lift up The Nation of Israel and the Holy Temple, the Prime Minister of Israel and its' Officials. I plead the blood of Jesus over The Nation of Israel and the Holy Temple. I pray for the protection of the Prime Minister and their military force. I thank you Father that you are their shield and buckler, triumphing over every battle and that their Angel's are at the front line pushing back the forces that are trying to overtake them. I thank you Father that Israel rise above the enemy attacks and that you equip Israel's Army with everything they need to conquer. I cast down every terrorist group and I command their destruction. I rebuke Satan's attack against Israel, the Holy Temple and the Prime Minister.

I pray for a rise of a great Army out of Israel and the support of the United State of American, China, France and Canada. I pray that these army forces come together to battle against terrorist groups and any force that comes against Israel. And I thank you that because they bless Israel you will bless them exceedingly.

For Your Word states in Genesis 12:3; I will bless those who bless you, and whoever curses you I will curse; and all peoples on earth will be blessed through you."

And now Father, I thank you for an outpouring of Your Spirit on Your Holy Nation – Israel in the power and authority of Jesus' Name, Amen!

- God Bless Israel -

# Part Four

## Salvation Prayer

It is through Jesus that we receive eternal life and it is through the finished work of Jesus that we receive abundant life in the Earth. The Word of God says, "no one comes to the Father, unless they come through Jesus. Another passage states, "if you confess Jesus with your mouth and believe in your heart that God raised Him from the dead, you will be saved".

It is as simple as speaking, believing and receiving. Therefore, if you would like to receive the promises of God through His only begotten Son, Jesus, please pray the prayer of Salvation with me:

*Dear Heavenly Father, thank you for loving me and for giving me your only begotten Son Jesus who died on the cross. It is through His shed blood my sins are forgiven and it is through the finish work on the cross, I am delivered. Dear Heavenly Father, come into my life and save me now. I confess with my mouth the Lord Jesus and believe in my heart that Jesus rose from the grave and through His finished work on the cross I am saved. Thank you for hearing my prayers and for answering my prayers, and I believe that right now my name is written in the Lamb's book of life. Amen!*

# Daily Reading

*Scripture Reading To Healing Prayers*          Ephesians 3:14-21

*"Now to Him who is able to do far more abundantly than all that we ask or think, according to the power at work within us."*

Ephesians 3:14-21

# INFILLING OF THE HOLY SPIRIT PRAYER

Before Jesus ascended into Heaven, he told the disciples in John 14:16 he would give us a comforter that He may abide with us forever. Jesus further mentions, the Comforter is a Gift to assist us to spread the Gospel. In Acts 1:1-5,8 the Holy Spirit came on the scene approximately 52 days after Jesus' resurrection; Jesus says; "But you will receive power when the Holy Spirit comes upon you, and you will be my witnesses in Jerusalem, throughout Judea and Samaria, and to the ends of the earth." Holy Spirit is our Power the Anointing that helps us to fulfill our purpose and the finished work of Jesus Christ in the Earth. Without the anointing we are weak and unproductive. When the Holy Spirit reveals himself, it causes us to speak in spiritual tongues; it is out of our control. There is no need to be alarmed by him, but welcome him; receive the gift of the

Holy Spirit openly because it is our spiritual language that allows us to communicate with our creator and Father.

Speaking in tongues is the most controversial spiritual gift – it is our connection to God and our power against the attacks of our enemy – Satan.

If you have not received the infilling of the Holy Spirit, I welcome you to do so now, by repeating this prayer.

*Dear Heavenly Father, I ask that You release the fullness of Your Holy Spirit to flood the places vacated by the darkness in my mind, body and soul. Please fill me with Your precious Holy Spirit who gives me wisdom and instruction. I thank you for Your joy, Your peace, Your gentleness, Your goodness, Your meekness, Your faithfulness and Your self-control. Just as you filled the church in Acts with the Holy Spirit, I ask that you anoint me with the power that I will speak with other tongues. Your word states, for he that speaketh in an unknown tongue speaketh not unto men, but unto God: for no man understandeth him; howbeit in the Spirit he speaketh mysteries. And they were all filled with the Holy Ghost, and began to speak with other tongues, as the Spirit gave them utterance. Father God, I release my faith right now, I believe I receive a spiritual language as the Spirit gives me utterance and I thank you for the infilling of the Holy Spirit, right now – in the name of Jesus! Amen.*

Congratulation! You now have the infilling of the Holy Spirit. To develop your spiritual language, practice speaking in your spiritual language daily. To do this you have to initiate the process by automatically speaking in your prayer language. It may sound like gibberish at the beginning but as you practice it daily, just as you practice playing a sport, you will perfect it and it will begin to become natural to you. Praise God!

Again, congratulations on the decision to make Jesus your Lord and Savior and for receiving the gift of the Holy Spirit that will help you ignite the power that is in you, on you and flowing through you in order to successfully accomplish your divine destiny.

- Know that the Power of God is with you always -

# Daily Reading

*Scripture Reading To Healing Prayers*           1 Peter 5

*"Therefore humble yourselves under the mighty hand of God, that He may exalt you in due time, casting all your care upon Him, for He cares for you."*

1 Peter 5:6-7

# ABOUT
# HEALING TODAY MINISTERS

This ministry is founded on the principles of Jesus and His finished work on the cross. It is an offspring to Healing Today Broadcast Ministries, which is a prophetic healing ministry broadcasted weekly on your local Christian cable station. For more information on the ministries and how you can partner and support this ministry, do visit our website at www.healingtoday.net where you have the opportunity to partake of more resources.

It is my prayer that the Grace of God be with you and His love manifest in your life - through the crucifixion and finish work of Jesus Christ, the Messiah and the only begotten Son of God, be with you forever. Amen

## Prayer Request

As a partner of this ministry the most important benefit is us joining our Faith with you in prayer.

Email your prayer request to:
www.livingwordministries@netzero.net
or
www.healingtoday.net

Be sure to send your testimonies to the ministry once you receive the manifestation of what you have been praying for.

## Donations to the Ministry

This ministry depends on donations. Please visit our website at www.healingtoday.net to partner and support the ministry of Jesus Christ.

## Order Copies for Bulk Retail Distribution
www.livingwordpublishing.net

Healing Today is dedicated to promoting Health and Wealth for the body of Christ. Please be sure to visit our website often for more empowering resources and new releases.

# Coming Soon!

Law of Attraction: The Power in "I AM "I Have "I Believe" 100 Wealth Building Affirmations to Ignite the Power Within You and Achieve Healing, Success, Wealth, Joy, Abundance and Prosperity is coming in June 2015.

This powerful book on affirmations is sure to attract wealth for a more prosperous life.

## Order Your Copy Today!

### www.amazon.com
### or
### www.healingtoday.net

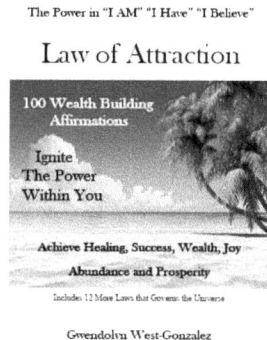

The Power in "I AM" "I Have" "I Believe"

Law of Attraction

100 Wealth Building Affirmations

Ignite The Power Within You

Achieve Healing, Success, Wealth, Joy Abundance and Prosperity

Includes 12 More Laws that Govern the Universe

Gwendolyn West-Gonzalez